Making Money From Crypto Currency

Christopher J Collins

Copyright © 2018 Christopher J Collins

All rights reserved.

ISBN-13: 978-1983619793
ISBN-10: 1983619795

DEDICATION

Dedicated to the fathers and mothers who do what they can to earn an income from home.

CONTENTS

	Disclaimer	i
1	Are you looking for an easy way to get started with Crypto Currency? You don't need thousands of dollars to buy a Bitcoin.	8
2	Method 1 - Invest	Pg 9
3	Method 2 - Trade	Pg 14
4	Method 3 - Become An Affiliate	Pg 19

DISCLAIMER

The author accepts no liability for the investment decisions of the reader or others. The author accepts no liability for the third party services mentioned in this book. This book is merely intended as a simple guide for how to get started with crypto currency and the reader is responsible for their own due diligence checks of any crypto currency exchange they sign up for.

Never invest more than you can afford to lose.
Past performance is no guarantee of future results.
Investment returns may fluctuate and are subject to market volatility.
Investing in Crypto Currency involves risk, and there is always the potential of losing money when you invest in Crypto Currency.

Crypto Currency is coming under increasing regulation and scrutiny. It is the reader's responsibility to ensure that their activities in Crypto Currency investment and trading are lawful within the relevant jurisdictions.

ARE YOU LOOKING FOR AN EASY WAY TO GET STARTED WITH CRYPTO CURRENCY?

YOU DON'T NEED THOUSANDS OF DOLLARS TO BUY A BITCOIN

If you are a Crypto Currency virgin and want to get started then this book is for you. There is no need to be afraid of the dark web or getting scammed. Some of the most visited and trusted websites in the world now deal in Crypto Currency they are called Crypto Currency Exchanges where you can buy, sell and transfer crypto currency.

There are lots of Crypto Currency Exchanges on the internet and many of them are extremely simple to get started. Crypto Currency Exchanges such as Coinbase are actually really user intuitive. Within a matter of minutes you can signup with your email address, upload your scanned id documents, link your bank or credit / debit card details and you are ready to go.

How do people make money with Crypto Currency Exchanges ? There are three methods I will discuss here which ALL involve the use of TRUSTED CRYPTO CURRENCY EXCHANGES.

METHOD 1 - INVEST

The simplest way to get started with Crypto Currency is investing. You simply buy crypto currency at a crypto currency exchange, do nothing with it and hope it will increase in value to sell at a future date.

Some noted investors predict the crash of crypto currency and the Bitcoin bubble, while others such as John McAffee predict the value of a single Bitcoin will rise above $500,000 by the year 2020. It is not my place to give you financial speculation of whether you will profit from an investment in crypto currency or not. I am just trying to illustrate the scale of the potential opportunities and make them accessible to you. It is certainly not considered too late by many to invest in crypto currency now. See example below given by Ali Sheikh https://medium.com/@alisheikh/thanksgiving-crypto-question-of-the-year-is-it-too-late-to-get-into-cryptos-5c3941ee107e

---

On 11/20/2017 Bitcoin's price was **$8,244.69**

If you bought 1 Bitcoin,

3 months ago: $4,066.60 / *103% return*

6 months ago: $2,040.18 / *304% return*

12 months ago: $728.51 / *1032% return*

As of 11/20/2017 Ethereum's price was **$367.71**

If you bought 1 Ethereum,

3 months ago: $298.20 / 23% return

6 months ago: $123.06 / 199% return

12 months ago: $9.57 / 3742% return

As of, 11/20/2017 Litecoin's price was **$72.38**,

If you bought 1 Litecoin,

3 months ago: $45.81 / 58% return

6 months ago: $27.42 / 164% return

12 months ago: $3.88 / 1765% return

The point Ali Sheikh makes *'not saying that these trends will continue (and not saying that they will not), the point is that the further you delay the more you are going to wish you got in yesterday'*

I wrote this book to help beginners who are interested in investing make an easy safe purchase of Crypto Currency. You don't need to get bamboozled by a geeky person in the free ads or go looking for advice from a techy friend of a friend you just sign up to a TRUSTED CRYPTO CURRENCY

EXCHANGE such as coinbase.com, and start with a buy of a small value of crypto currency spending an amount of what you can afford to lose.

Once you have registered with a TRUSTED CRYPTO CURRENCY EXCHANGE such as Coinbase.com you will be ready to buy and sell Crypto Currency, it is that simple. Simple investing is buying at current price on one crypto currency exchange (e.g. coinbase) and holding the investment there until the value rises in the future and then selling (also see METHOD 2 - Trading)

Coinbase.com has a really simple Dashboard

Click on the tabs to see the market trends for Bitcoin/Bitcoin Cash/Ethereum/Litecoin

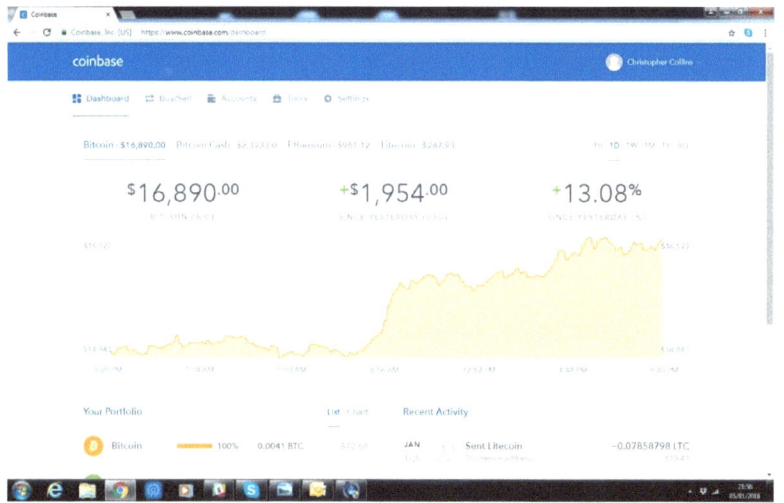

Coinbase has a simple Buy/Sell functionality

Once you have linked your card details simply type the amount you are prepared to invest in Bitcoin/Bitcoin Cash/Ethereum/Litecoin

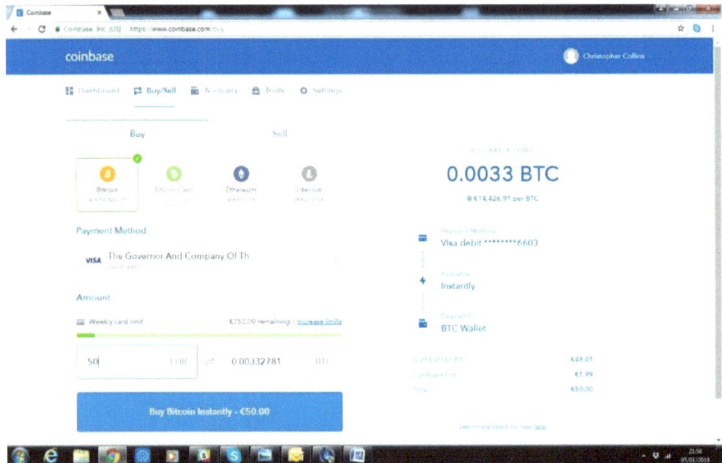

You don't need thousands of dollars to buy a Bitcoin or hundreds of dollars to buy a Litecoin. At Crypto Currency Exchanges you can buy the value of a percentage of a coin. Your first investment in crypto currency doesn't have to be a significant amount of money. My first purchase of crypto currency was $50 worth of Litecoin from Coinbase , representing a percentage of a value of a Litecoin, my second purchase was $50 worth of Bitcoin from Coinbase. Later I decided to move my Litecoin from Coinbase.com to Coinegg.com where I decided to use the value of it to purchase an emerging Crypto Currency called XLM.

How do you know if you can trust a crypto currency exchange? I often use Alexa.com to do research of websites. According to Alexa.com, Coinbase is currently the 270th most visited website in the world and 42nd most visited website in the United States. Next I checked whois.com to find out who was the registered owner of the website, from there you can see who is the registered business owner and company name holding the website, you can then do further due diligence checks on the company. There are many due diligence checks that you can carry out on the company entity and domain owner of the website.

When dealing with Crypto Currency Exchanges be prepared to spend a small commission in making the purchase, sales, account withdrawals.

What crypto currency should I invest in? According to cryptocoincharts.info there are at least 125 Crypto Currency Exchanges . According to wikipedia there are over 1381 crypto currencies and the number is growing. You have to do your own research on them. There are two investment approaches. You can either invest in the mainstream ones or you can invest in the emerging ones. Consider however if you were wanting to double your money on Bitcoin today you would need to see its value rise from 15k to 30k, whereas the trading price of smaller currencies such as XLM would only need to double in value from a few cents to few dollars for you to double your investment.

METHOD 2 - TRADE

METHOD 2 - TRADE - You buy crypto currency at a low price on one exchange, transfer it to another crypto currency exchange and sell it at a higher price.

SENDING CRYPTO CURRENCY FROM ONE EXCHANGE TO ANOTHER

Ok so you have made your first purchase of crypto currency on coinbase and you want to send the crypto currency to another exchange where you can sell it for money (This website shows you which exchanges may pay you more https://coinmarketcap.com/currencies/litecoin/#markets)

Go to the Accounts tab of Coinbase.com and click on Send button of relevant wallet e.g. Bitcoin / Bitcoin Cash / ETH / Litecoin

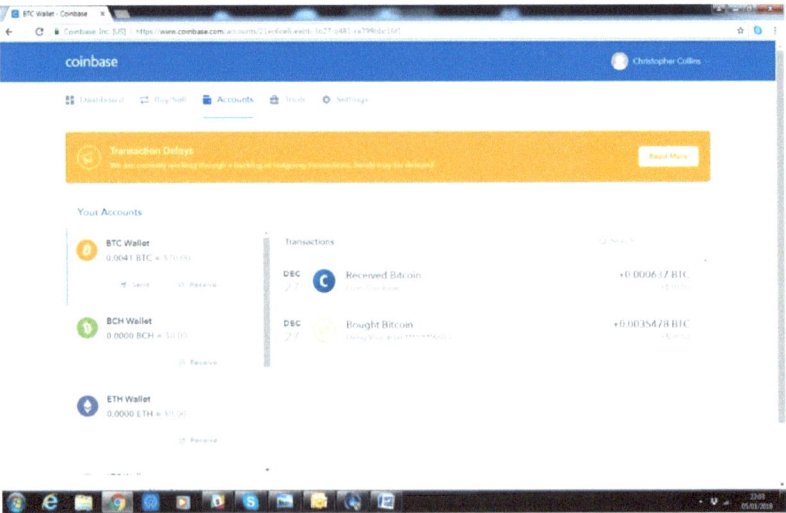

2. You will be prompted to add a Recipient address

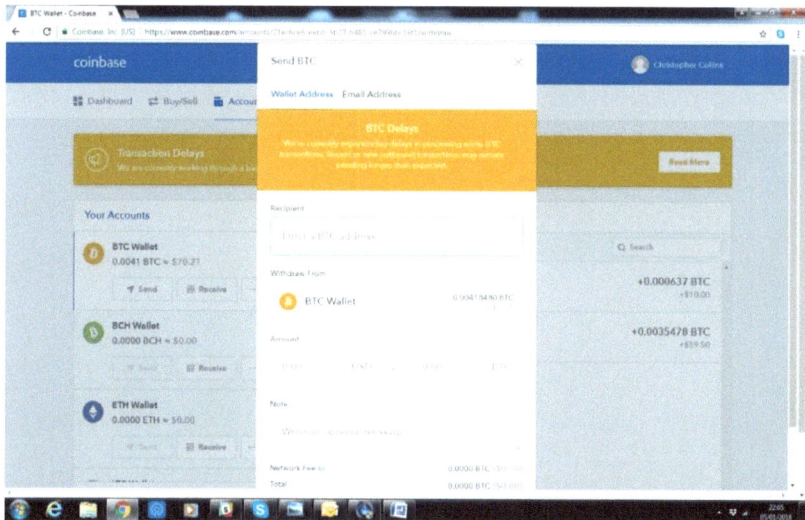

3. Go to another crypto currency exchange e.g. coinegg.com and get wallet address

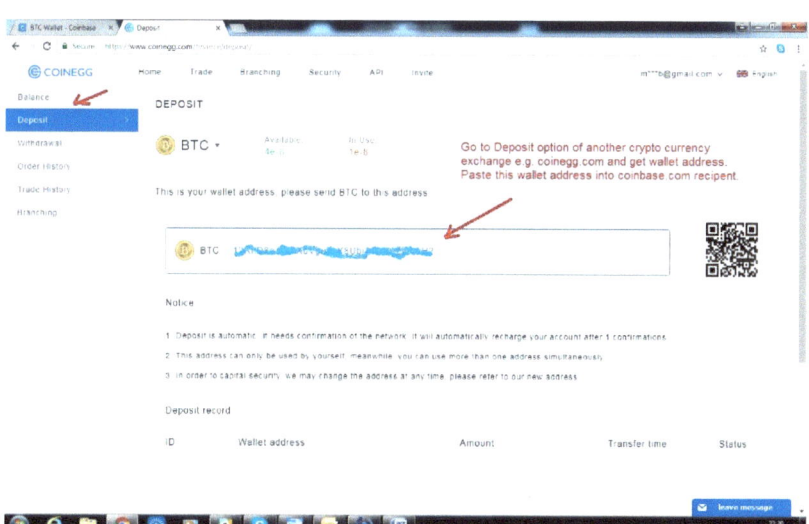

4. Paste the other exchange wallet address into coinbase.com, if you are ok with the Network fee, enter the amount you are transferring and click Continue to send the currency from one exchange to another.

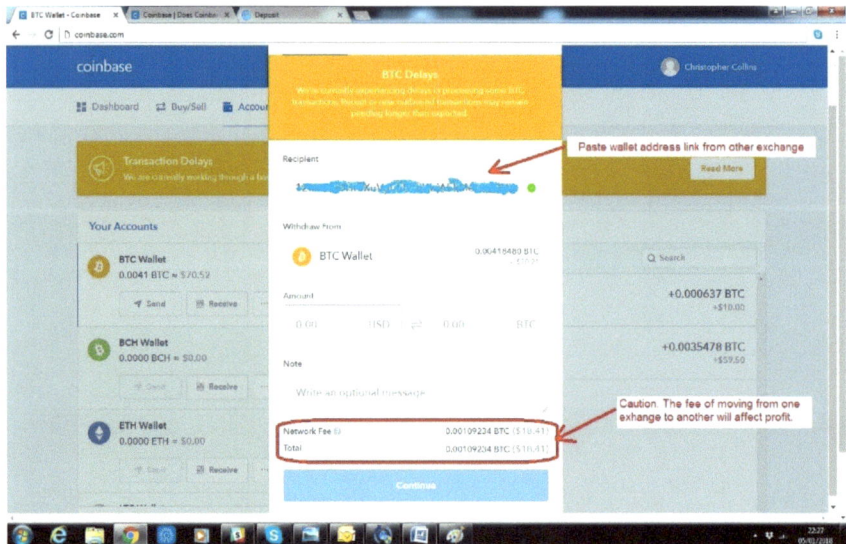

CAUTION: CHECK THE TRANSFER CHARGES

The process of moving crypto currency from one exchange to another is extremely simple. However as I discovered if you try to move Bitcoin from Coinbase to CoinEgg, Gatecoin or OkCoin. The receiving exchange may try to charge you a transfer fee of as much as $16 - $17 on the transaction. When I moved Litecoin from Coinbase to CoinEgg I was only charged a few cents for the transfer.

When I first looked into this Litecoin was trading at $245 on one exchange and selling for $369 on another exchange. There were significant profits to be made from moving one exchange to another. However it can take 1 or 2 days to get your account verified on each crypto currency exchange that you join.

Click the following link to see the disparity of Litecoin prices between various exchanges

https://coinmarketcap.com/currencies/litecoin/#markets

Below are some examples of price variance that I found between different exchanges on the 24th December 2017

BTC-Alpha LTC/USD $245.28

WEX LTC/USD $259.22

Exmo LTC/USD $273.00

BitFlip LTC/USD $290.00

BitKonan LTC/USD $298.50

YoBit LTC/USD $315.20

Gatecoin LTC/USD $369.00

You will need to join lots of Crypto Currency Exchanges so that you will always be ready to take advantage of the opportunity of when one exchange is buying and selling at a higher price than another.

You need to be prepared to spend a small commission in making the purchase, sales, transfers from one exchange to another, withdrawals from final exchange of sale. This method of making a profit from crypto currency is only really possible if you are dealing in volumes where there is a profit left after all the charges.

METHOD 3 - BECOME AN AFFILIATE

You can also earn money from Crypto Currency Exchanges by referring friends to this safe method of buying and selling crypto currencies.

Most currency exchanges have an Invite friends option. On coinbase it is located just below your profile link

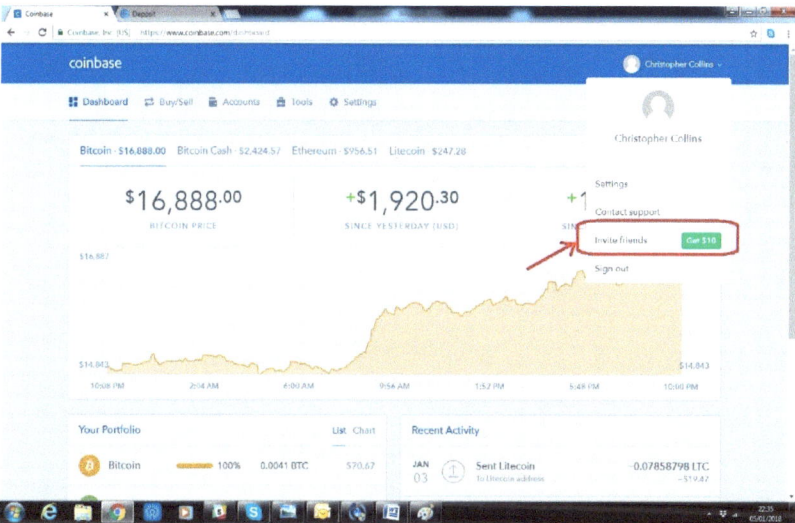

Here is where you can find your affiliate link and share it with others to make money/free crypto currency credit.

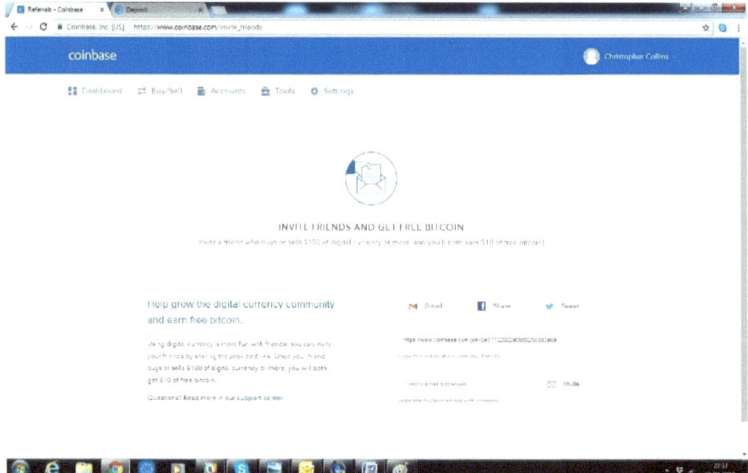

Examples of affiliate rewards and offers

Coinbase - INVITE FRIENDS AND GET FREE BITCOIN - Invite a friend who buys or sells $100 of digital currency or more, and you'll both earn $10 of free bitcoin!
https://www.coinbase.com/join/5a3772202298b8025c8d3a09

Coinegg - you will receive 30% as commission of the transaction fee within 6 months from the date of your friend's registration.

Gatecoin For a limited time only, you can claim US$10 to trade bitcoin by signing up to Gatecoin.com. Gatecoin enables you to trade bitcoins in more than 40 countries. It is easy to use, reliable and secured. Enjoy! Use referal code **NJQIEH** to enjoy this offer.

If you would like a system the frequently shares your affiliate link with hashtag intelligence to social media, I recommend you check out https://www.tweet-eye.com/

Start by joining an exchange such as Coinbase and Coinegg right now and use a FREE plan on Tweet-Eye.com to promote your affiliate links on social media.

Tweet-Eye.com is a simple and easy to use tool to schedule and automate sending your affiliate links to social media accounts and with built in hashtag intelligence and geo location tools helps find your target market.

- Easily connects to Twitter, Tumblr, Facebook, LinkedIn and Pinterest
- Free up your precious time. Schedule and automate your social media posts.
- Use Marketing Assistant feature to find your customers on social media.

ABOUT THE AUTHOR

Christopher Collins has a law degree from Aberystwyth University. He has a passion to help others discover ethical methods to make money online.

He is Director of Picality Limited and is designer of Tweet Eye software that helps buyers and sellers make money online.

Many people wonder if it is too late to get into cryptos. In this short guide Christopher will give you three simple methods to consider if you don't want to miss out on the opportunities of the Crypto Currency revolution. He says it is 'Easy to start and it is never too late'. You can be up and running in a matter of minutes.

NOTES

www.ingramcontent.com/pod-product-compliance
Lightning Source LLC
Chambersburg PA
CBHW041946240526
45473CB00033B/621